INTELLIGENT DESIGN IN SCIENCE, RELIGION AND YOU

INTELLIGENT DESIGN IN SCIENCE, RELIGION AND YOU

Nickolas Bay

To order additional copies of this book, contact:
Xlibris Corporation
1-888-795-4274
www.Xlibris.com
Orders@Xlibris.com
36274

CONTENTS

Prologue... 11
Foreword... 13
Who, What, Where Is God?.. 17
Science And Religion What Is Living Matter? 18
One God . . . Comparative Religions Agree........................ 20
A New World—A Religious Democracy............................. 24
Fictitious Scenario # 2 Religions Agree On Sin And Repentance........... 31
Theology Vs. Atheism 40
The Seven Sins... 42
The Seven Virtues 43
The Authors Own Comments Continue
Beyond The Unified Field Theory 46
Politics And Religion 48
Reviewing Religious Doctrines 49
The Quabbala, The Secret Doctrine Of Israel 52
Science Illustrated In ThE Book Of Genesis 54
Buddhism 57
Mahayana Buddhism 58
Zoroastrianism 59
Confucianism 61
Christianity 62
The Apostolic Age 63
Islam 64
Muslim Beliefs 65
The Ancient Catholic Church 67
Sikhism 69
The Protestant Reformation And Its Catholic Counterpart 70
The Church In The Modern World 71
Questions To Ponder 72
The Key To Survival 73
When Does Life Start? 79
Brain, Mind, Soul And The Spirit 82
Where Do We Look For God? 85

There Is Nothing New 87
Here's A Hypothetical 89
We Are All DescendanTs Of One God 91
For A Quick Reference To Religions 92

Dedicated to

Miriam, my lifetime love and partner.

Books by Nickolas Bay

Genetic Swaps an Ethical Dilemma

The Chameleon Project DNA

Without Firing a Shot

God Is In Your Molecules

Sonny, the Immigrants' Son

Secret Research at the CIA

Intelligent Design in Science, Religion and You. (Part I)

Intelligent Design in science, Religion and You (Revised edition)

Gene Research at the CIA

It Will Come About In Silence: USA forced to use its Secret WMD

PROLOGUE

The text begins with asking if God belongs to a particular religion or if he is partial to a political party. Parallels on where various religions agree are stressed rather than where they differ. Comparisons begin with the beliefs of primitive people and those of religious orders over the past four thousand years.

The author presents a scenario that brings leaders of six major religions together to agree on reality. Questions are asked and answered by these religious leaders questioning how intelligent design works in their religion.

Eighteen questions are given the reader to compare his or her beliefs with what they think they know about their religion and perhaps their prejudices of other religions.

The composite of the books ideas are brought together under the heading, "The Key to Survival." Intelligent Design points out that the molecular design of the universe is the basis and confirmation for religious beliefs.

FOREWORD

This story begins at the beginning, Genesis, pointing out the sameness in all of us and the rest of creation. We begin with the atom and molecular nature of all things in the universe. We and all of our surroundings are made of the same material. This lays the ground work affirming one God for all religious beliefs.

Several religious doctrines are reviewed from ancient worship to contemporary times. The similarity in all these religions from recorded time are pointed out and made obvious by their own words. The ultimate proposal in the text is to ask the many religions in today's world to acknowledge there is one creator. We have been created under scientific formulas that make it obvious we are all made of the same material, molecules.

Science is shown as the logical approach to unravel nature's secrets. Science is that part of religion that helps us express what we see as reality. Religion should work hand in hand with science. Disclosing the creator's formulas for life through science will bring us closer to understanding who we are and why, as a brotherhood of mankind, we should show "mutuality" when dealing with each other.

Science is the proof of Intelligent Design.

PART I

WHO, WHAT, WHERE IS GOD?

Is God a Jew, Catholic, Islamist, Taoist, Protestant, Buddhist, Hindu, Shinto, Zoroastrian, Republican, Independent or Democrat? Perhaps God is a conservative or a liberal? God is all of the above and then some. But God is not just one of them.

Many religious ideologies have things in common. They lay down rules for moral and ethical daily living. They bring their followers together by teaching dogma and ritualistic ceremonies. They propose bringing all of the world's population into their religious beliefs. Unfortunately they believe they and their prophets have the exclusive path to salvation. The following are the author's feelings:

Who is God . . . . God is everything.

What is God . . . . God is the creative intelligence of the world.

Where is God? . . . God is all matter and non-matter.

If we can agree on one God, why can't we practice our religious beliefs as one way to the same Creator?

Look over the various ideologies in this text and see the similarity in our beliefs.

Find the common ground and think on it. Our problems today and in the past focus on our differences, let's now focus on our similarities and learn to live together peacefully.

SCIENCE AND RELIGION
WHAT IS LIVING MATTER?

People and animals breathe; when they stop breathing we say they are dead. Plants, grass and trees are alive as long as they continue with osmosis, when they stop we say they are dead. Most fish use gills to absorb oxygen, when this stops we say they are dead.

Molecules are the one thing in all living matter that remains in them as they live and after they die. Molecules never die. Molecules can change if their atomic structure changes but they do not die. The same applies to the atoms within the molecule. One of eighteen descriptions of life in Webster's Dictionary is, #13 . . . . Vigor, liveliness, animation, vivacity. A synonym of Live is exist, reside, subsist, continue, endure. Certainly atoms and molecules have life and they live. They do not have to breathe or use osmosis to subsist. If we concur that matter [molecules] is neither made or destroyed we have uncovered material life that has no death. Atoms can leave one molecule and join another but this is change, not death.

It follows then that when the sperm unites with the egg this is not the beginning of life since life is already in the composition of egg and sperm as molecules. The union of egg and sperm create a new molecular form, which after gestation becomes a new individual. The newborn child takes its first breath and begins molecular change on its own.

If atoms and molecules live forever, then is this not *"World without end?"* When we eat and drink our chemistry changes and molecular change becomes part of us. Each molecule adds to the physical substance of that person. If one claims atoms and molecules do not have spiritual content then we must assume the spirit is separate from the individual's molecular make-up. If this is so, when does the spirit enter the newborn baby? If the spirit enters the baby at its first breath then we have a molecular structure [spiritless] that becomes the physical foundation for a new spirit to occupy. While the fetus is growing in the mother's womb, we have the fetus subsisting from the molecules [food] of the mother. The mother has the spirit, so it doesn't seem logical that her molecules containing spirit are providing molecules to her fetus that has no spirit.

It is logical to propose that the mother's molecular system is producing a new molecular system within her. One spiritual being is creating another spiritual being.

ONE GOD . . . COMPARATIVE RELIGIONS AGREE

Intelligent design is God's Formula

Let's look at what all these religious ideologies have in common.

PRIMITIVE PEOPLE

They have the basic belief that there is a creator or supernatural force that makes the world and Universe work. Primitive people believe in Mana, an indwelling of power that can cause a kind of extraordinary action. They venerate plants and animals. They believe in a great God in the sky who makes everything, plants, animals and man.

God is the ultimate lawgiver and overseer. Death is viewed as a departure of a soul from its body, which it has directed during its lifetime. Today, science confirms this belief there's an indwelling of power in every molecule that does not die.

MOSES AND THE EARLY JEWISH RELIGION

In the secret doctrine of Israel: Quabbala, meaning the secret or hidden tradition of the unwritten law.

According to an early Rabbi it was delivered to man in order that he might learn to understand the mystery of the universe about him and the universe within him. To the writer this seems to point to the fact that science is disclosing these secrets. Molecules are without us and are within us, we are all one.

Genesis 2:7—And the Lord God formed man of the dust of the ground, and reached into his nostrils the breath of life; and man became a living soul. Is this not the same as molecules being rearranged to form molecules of a different formation—the human being? Is this not God's universal law that we term science today? Is this not an illustration of the compatibility of science and religion? Man was formed by materials already existing under God's Laws, dust of the ground. Man is created from molecular matter and this matter is the vehicle for the soul.

HINDUISM

The Way of Knowledge—Jnana Marga—more difficult than The Way of the Works. After 800 BC new rituals were brought about. All things men, animals, plants, come from one thing or being to which they return. Here again science has established grounds for this thinking of 800 BC. We are made up of a molecular structure of the universe and those molecules remain in the universe on our leaving it.

MAHAYANA BUDDHISM

ZEN

One must seek flashes of insight and reject systematic study and discussions. This is known as Satori in Japan. The oneness of the universal self is pre-supposed. All phenomena are alike in their Buddha essence. Here again we reveal science at work. All things in the universe are composed of the same molecular materials in different arrangements, making them the same but unique and different from each other.

TAOISM

Tao-Te-Ching wrote a treatise called, "Treatise on the Tao and its power." It says that all things come from nonbeing and return to nonbeing. Isn't this the same concept today when we say all things come from unseen molecules and return to unseen molecules upon our dying? This is science verifying ancient old beliefs.

It continues, the Sages know all things come from and blend into one and that they are themselves one with all things in the one. Again science agrees and confirms, in today's terms the universe is composed of untold trillions of molecules making the whole. Some molecules come from the whole configured as human beings, some as animals, some as plants, but all blend back into the universal whole because they never leave it.

CONFUCIUS

He taught Shu; do as one would be done by. Found today in the Christian's golden rule, "Do unto others as you would have others do unto you." Confucius felt he was designated by heaven to teach his doctrines of mutuality {Shu}.

CHRISTIANITY

Christians—God one father of all. Christians regard Jesus as an incarnation of God the Father and therefore the source of primary revelation. It follows that Jesus born of Mary walked this earth according to god's formulas' of molecular structure.

THE FIRST OF THE FIVE MUSLIM BELIEFS IS:

Allah is the one true God and does not share his divinity with any associate. It follows that Mohammad the prophet was born of a woman on this earth and lived according to molecular structure set up by intelligent design or Allah.

All these religions agree in God's existence or an intelligent design, but the problem arises when one religion thinks their religion is the only way to God. Let's pursue that idea.

WORD POWER AND SEARCHING FOR THE TRUTH

The oral word can be accented with voice inflections, tonal qualities and body language, but the written word stands on its own. Written words convey situations in the form of adjectives, verbs, nouns, pronouns etc. using tenses to explain when an action took place.

No word is absolutely descriptive. Words are always limited and qualified. The same word carries a different meaning for each individual. Interpretation of words in a different language distorts its meaning to a greater degree.

What is truth? The answer is (???????????). I dare say if we ask a thousand people to give their concept of truth we will have one thousand different opinions. Try this with your friends. When your friend says, after looking at a piece of material, "that's blue."

You look at the same material and say, no,' it's more of a purple. You are both right and wrong. Each perceives what they are constructed to see; in fact the material is made of many colors and they only see a predominate color. Each perceives via their own cornea which cannot be the same. The molecules making the structure of one person's eyes are not the same molecules making up the others eyes.

When Pontius Pilot asked Jesus, "What is Truth?" HE DID NOT ANSWER?

The truth we seek is in the Holy Spirit which abides in everyone. Human explanations are merely perceptions and approximations of ones thoughts via brain, mind, and soul. Our human experiences brought about by individual choice are relayed via brain, mind, soul and finally to our Holy Spirit. Absolute truth or perfection cannot be comprehended by our limited existence. When each person has turned inwardly and finally becomes one with the Holy Spirit then and only then will the full truth be known. We will have returned to the uncaused cause where we originated. At that time worldly thoughts like ego, desire, greed, and all other human emotions will play no part in distorting what is real.

The truth in our lifetime cannot be revealed, every one of us is special and different from the other. No two humans see the same thing exactly the same. That is impossible since our perception comes from a material body that is unique to itself. Asking someone for the truth is like asking someone to fly by beating his or her arms up and down. We are not equipped to fly and we are not constructed in our present form to know the truth.

The pursuit of truth is a good thing as is the striving for perfection, but we must have the ability to put ourselves in the shoes of another who does not agree with us in this endeavor. Eliminating any one who does not agree with our religious or political beliefs does not make our ideas true. Eliminating Jesus did not make the Romans right, just as forcing a person to convert to Islam or kill them does not make the extreme Islamist right.

A NEW WORLD—A RELIGIOUS DEMOCRACY

A FICTITIOUS SCENARIO

Six people representing six different religions are sitting across from each other around a long mahogany table, three on one side and three on the other. Each has the belief that his or her concept of God, or the original source, is absolute. The host and moderator holds up a pair of glasses and explains that they were designed through an advanced state of Nanotechnology.

"My friends I have a pair of glasses for each of you but before I pass them out I must warn you these are not ordinary glasses. When you put them on you will all see the same thing at the same time, reality." The learned people look at each other and give the moderator a polite smile."

"When you put these glasses on don't be shocked, they will not hurt you in any way." He then put on a pair to demonstrate they were merely glasses and not harmful. Everyone's curiosity is aroused and they eagerly reach for their pair of glasses. Before handing them out the moderator instructs each person to look at the person directly across the table from him, then look slowly at all the other participants in the room. "Please look for the obvious difference in each individual."

He hands out the glasses. Each person puts the glasses on and immediately a collective gasp fills the room. All are startled and amazed, unsure of what they are seeing.

A Rabbi is asked by the moderator, "Rabbi, what do you see as you look through the glasses?"

He replies, "All I see are millions of swirling dots." The moderator walks around the room and asks each person what they see. The replies are all the same. Then he asks each one to look at all of the other people in the room and tell him if there is any difference in the patterns from one person to the next . . . . all reply . . . . "There are no differences."

Father McCormick, a Catholic priest asks, "What are we supposed to be seeing?"

The moderator replies," These glasses have been designed to reduce everything we see to their molecular make-up. Look again from person to person, can anyone see a difference?" No-one could.

"The point here is simple. No matter what Religion we believe in we cannot ignore the fact that we are all made up of the same material. Let's look at the Old Testament, Genesis 2:17 And the Lord God formed man of the dust of the ground, and breathed into his nostrils the breath of life; and man became a living soul."

"So we begin with what we have in common. We are all created from molecules of dust and we return to the same after death. We have many skin colors in this room, one black person, one brown, one yellow and three white. When you look through your glasses you see no color distinction, correct?" All present agreed.

He continues, "We are all part of the same creative force. If you look around the room you will only see molecular energy. If you were to look at animals or birds or minerals through your glasses you would see the same thing. It is obvious we are all made of the same matter. After death we are still a form of molecular matter. I put the question to you, why is your religion the only way?" There is only one God or original source, yet we all espouse our religion is the only true path to the creator of Intelligent Design. Prophets from all religions share the same molecular make-up that we all do today."

"Science has proven that our energy content can be increased by our mental ability and thought process. We know for example that our serotonin level can increase by merely smiling at someone. In fact experiments have shown people in the same room will increase their serotonin level even when an act of kindness is expressed to someone else in the room."

"Good feelings are not felt when we are ostracized or rebuked no matter what religion we profess. We now have a handle on reality and how our actions and thought processes change what we perceive as real. We express reality in the way we see things. If we all were able to see the same thing at the same time and that sight was seen through these molecular glasses reality would be the same to us all. But, you say, religious beliefs are based on faith not reality. True, but faiths are based on what other people have seen or experienced or said. As you have just experienced the only way all of us can see the same thing at the same time is to look at reality through unprejudiced molecular vision. As soon as we take the glasses off our cognitive powers become obscured with personal prejudices and beliefs, which create barriers that prevent us from understanding another person's point of view or beliefs. All religions require blind faith from their followers as the bottom line that separates the believers from the non-believers".

"It is obvious that our innate creative force can be used to change real manifestations and the thoughts of others. Is it not fair to conclude that we are all part of one creative force and that this force has the on going power to create change in both physical and thought processes?"

"Religions have played an important part in the growth of social order; the problem however, is that with religious evolution came exclusiveness due to geography and social needs. Today this is evidenced in many religions such as Catholicism, Judaism, Mohammadism, Hinduism, Buddhism, and Protestantism as represented by the religious representatives in this room. Of course there are many other religious beliefs, the list goes on and on. All profess they are the true path or the only way to Nirvana or heaven and that their God is the only true God. This belief of course has led to religious wars and bloodshed as far back as recorded time."

"I believe there are many paths to the creator. The fact is they all lead to the same God. As you have witnessed today we are all part of a universal creative force. Why then can't our numerous religions get together and agree on the one truth we have just witnessed, we are all the same and all will return to the creator of all."

"One religion is not better than another. All religions, in one way or another, follow rules for living in what they espouse as a proper life. The essential change will be to eliminate the doctrine that one religion is the only way to heaven. Religions are formed from social needs in their geographic areas and this will not change. What a wonderful life if all religions worked together, keeping their own identity but working together for the common good of humankind . . . under one God." A sort of religious democracy.

The Rabbi says; "If we are all the same how do you explain our individualism and differences in personalities?"

"Good question Rabbi, we are all made of the same molecular material, we surely agree on that fact. Your molecules are not mine, nor anyone else's in the universe, they're unique to you. Your DNA evolved from many, many molecular changes since the beginning of time. You are what you are as the result of those changes. Every grain of sand on the beach is different; every snowflake is different."

"If we have three apples, one yellow, one green and one red, they are obviously different in characteristics making them unique. Now, if I crush them and make applesauce out of them, there is no trace of their original appearance, they are now seen as they are in their present state. The taste and characteristics of the applesauce is unlike any of the individual apples, it has a taste and shape of its own. It is more than the apples it took to make it. We perceive an object or person in the state they are presently in, which was caused by the culmination of events over time."

"Gestalt psychologists have the right idea in saying that the whole is not the sum of its parts, it is more than each part and more than their total. Look at the similarity, the 6th Century B.C. Taoist Lao-Tzu said, 'All things come from and blend into one and they are themselves one with all things in the one.'"

The Protestant priest says, "That's an interesting premise. What is your theory on why some people are born with physical problems and others not?"

"I know, some people are quick to blame God for their problems. I believe the universe is the only perfect thing there is. The Creator set up universal laws, which encompass all those laws directing our planet and the activities of outer space and of the constantly expanding universe. We, as humans, have evolved because our changes were in tune with those universal laws. Faraday, Maxwell and Einstein have only scratched the surface."

"If someone is born with a physical problem their molecular composition was working in accordance with the creator's laws. We humans look at this person as incomplete by our concepts of what is 'normal.' In some cases we can change the genetic order of that person's genre and their "abnormality" to what we perceive as normal. If these changes were made contrary to creations formulas or laws they would not work."

"Many abnormalities can be repaired by genetic replacements today. This does not make us Gods, and we are not meddling with God's laws. I submit we are working within God's laws and that is the only reason genetic replacements work. Bringing someone's gene balance in line to make them healthy is proof that we are in tune with the Creator's laws."

"We, at this time in the evolution of man, have been given the insight to understand and use some of the formulas of creation. We are not creating new laws we are discovering laws that have always existed. James Watson and his associate, Crick who discovered the DNA molecule's double—helix structure, didn't create the DNA system they discovered it."

"Jet airplanes, computers and televisions are only three examples of how humans have discovered and applied creative formulas that exist in the universe today. These formulas existed before we "discovered" them; they existed 2000 years ago. Cell phones and televisions would have worked in those days but those discoveries were yet to come."

"Falling from God's grace, I believe, is making decisions contrary to the Creator's pre-set laws for life. A man and woman unite; his sperm fertilizes the female's egg, two molecular entities unite to form a third molecular form. A man's sperm or a woman's egg alone does not produce new life. It takes a combination of molecular union to produce new life that has properties of both sexes, but is different than both."

"Life continues by change of molecular arrangements, which are formed within the formulas of the creator's grand design. The formulas continue to operate after what we term 'death.'"

"We continue to be molecular after death. We can speculate that there is a chronicle of our life in our molecular make-up as there are experiences recorded in our DNA. Our molecules combine with others to become new particles of matter. Life forces continue to emerge as new forms of energy."

"One could look at the cycle of creation starting with death, at which time our molecular nature changes. Vegetables and fruit begin as small molecular forms that when exposed to the right conditions: air, water and sunlight, also molecular forms combine with these elements and grow. They are growing because their molecular form integrates with other molecular forms to create, what we perceive as a new form. In fact we are looking at molecules combining with other molecules to become a new form."

"When humans, animals, fish or fowl eat they are ingesting molecules and integrating them into their systems to survive. The food becomes part of their internal and external anatomy. A pregnant woman feeds her fetus by giving it nutrition, which is molecular in its own right and combines with the fetus's molecules which we see as physical growth. Sperm from the male unite with the egg of the female, both different in molecular nature and we have a new molecular form, which we eventually see as a baby.

No one religion can create or destroy that which is indestructible, the truth.

We have all heard that when a butterfly beats its wings in China the results are felt in North America and other parts of the world. Let us consider applying this thesis, that the universe is made of atoms and molecules all operating under an unbreakable supernatural law. The butterfly is beating its wings and displaces air molecules. This movement is added to the billions of movements by humans, animals, fish and fowl all over the earth at the same second. A massive molecular movement is created with effects felt worldwide, perhaps as weather changes. A miracle? No, all forces working under the same laws."

The Hindu monk asks, "How does your theory apply to meditation and prayer?"

"A good question let us consider the power of prayer. We know that neutrinos entering our body at the proper angle will create new matter. We know that these neutrinos are penetrating our planet and bodies every second of the day. We know that certain circumstances must prevail or the neutrinos will simply pass through our bodies, make no changes and do no apparent harm."

"When someone prays, emotional effects are felt. Is it not possible then that a molecular change is taking place in the body? This molecular change can make our body's atoms receptive to the neutrinos that are always present. New actions can then be made by the praying individual that are brought about by prayer and may well be beneficial to him or her."

"Well, you say how does that help the person being prayed for? We know that the brain gives off waves. Is it possible that prayers directed at an individual can actually permeate their body and cause molecular actions that set up an environment to receive neutrinos that will create new molecules to grow new tissue and destroy old matter that has made the person sick? Not all prayers give what we term positive responses . . . . not because the creator says you live and you die but because the sick individual cannot change their molecular nature to be receptive to neutrinos to create molecular change."

"These are all possibilities that certainly re-in force the fact that we are all made of the same stuff, molecules that when properly arranged contain the potential to create new matter. Creation meaning the re-aligning of the creative force potential in all of us, we are not producing something from nothing."

"Everything is . . . it is our destiny to discover "new" [to us], universal laws through science that will eventually bring mankind together. Science will not separate us from religion; it will merge us with religion."

The Buddhist monk asks the question, "How does one explain the power of will, or choice that mankind has if we think of everything from a molecular point of view. Molecules can't make choices."

. "An excellent question, here are my thoughts. Over unknown periods, of what we term as time, trillions of molecules have developed to the point that "man" was given the power of awareness and the ability to make choices. At that point of molecular development the supernatural force, God, set his plan in action to have human creation perpetuate itself ad finitum. The bible portrays this as the Garden of Eden. Adam and Eve were the first human molecular forces to be given the power to procreate an off-spring by uniting themselves via sperm and egg to reproduce what God had produced . . . human beings. God did not wave his hand and say produce a child . . . . They could only procreate by using Gods laws, which were to unite molecular form with molecular form to bring about a new molecular form, which we call a baby. These laws were followed when Jesus was born to Mary. God did not violate his own laws; Jesus was born through Gods pre-set laws of molecular change. Jesus did not appear from thin air, he was born under the pre-set natural laws of the Creator."

"Adam and Eve were the only molecular forms to reach the point of transition awareness. Animals, birds, fish, trees, rocks, and earth, all part of the grand plan and made up of the same molecules as Adam and Eve. Even if one does not believe in the story of Adam and Eve these principles remain the same. Today we live under the same scenario; we have fowl, animals, trees that are still made of the same molecular structure as they were years ago. To our knowledge, none have the power of will or awareness that humans have. Human beings can make choices based on what they perceive to be the outcome of such a choice based on past experiences. Human beings have books and libraries for reference, animals do not. As far as we know today animals cannot project into the future."

"You see evolution has a place in our thinking. You may or may not believe man evolved from apes. The point is that all things living and what we consider dead, have a molecular construction. Some highly sophisticated as man others as rocks elemental in comparison to man. There are no other molecular structures that we know of presently that have the will, awareness, and unique power of choice as man. Can monkeys and rocks evolve to man's level of molecular development? Up to now the answer is no. Everything in God's creation serves a purpose and has a relationship to everything else; this is obvious since we are all composed of the same types of molecules."

"It seems that religions separate us today more than unite us. Each produces fear in the other. God gave us the power of choice. We live in a universe based on the harmony of laws. We should exercise the privileges bestowed on us by realizing we are one family and continue to explore and discover the limitless laws of the universe. Jesus said,

"In my father's house are many mansions" . . . could he not have been referring to the limitless discoveries of the universe? Are we not all part of the mortar that holds the universe together? There is a place for every molecule in the universe regardless of our religious beliefs. One may argue that molecules may store memory but we have no proof they can think or make decisions. So this leads us to the next question. Does mankind have a spiritual essence or soul that directs his molecular being to operate by his or her choices? A mystic, Madam Blavatsky outlined spiritual growth taking place over many re-incarnations. A process designed to bring each person eventually into their soul's perfection, but only after going through limitless experiences in this world."

"Each one of the religions you represent also believes in a spiritual essence that guides your followers to make the right selections as dictated by your religion. Our basic differences then, come from each religion, which has its own unique ideological agenda. The Bahai's principal of faith, that includes harmony of science and religion is certainly a step in the right direction, to go a step farther, I believe science eventually will validate religion"

"Today different religious ideologies are the primary reason for international conflict. Hopefully, in the future, they will bring an understanding of one another and a world living under one creator's law of harmony."

"Each religion having respect for the other is a good starting point."

Gentlemen let us take a small break and return to discuss Sin and Repentance.

Every person is a miracle; you are the only one like you in the universe.

Fictitious Scenario # 2 RELIGIONS AGREE ON SIN AND REPENTANCE

The same six theologians were invited to discuss other religious interpretations to try to find a common ground in their theological beliefs. The idea was to take basic religious beliefs and compare them to see if they were different or alike in any way.

Let us begin with Islam's meaning of Repentance, would our honored guest the Imam form Saudi Arabia like to explain its meaning?

The Imam nods and says, "Tawbah is the word for repentance in Arabic; it literally means 'to return' and is mentioned in the Quran. In an Islamic context, it refers to the act of leaving what God has prohibited and returning to what He has commanded."

The moderator turns to the Rabbi, Rabbi, "How does the Torah cover Repentance?"

"I will be happy to highlight it for you. The Torah or the Mosaic Law which is based on the first five books of the Bible in Genesis makes distinctions between offenses against God and offenses against man. To confess one's sin before God it is essential the sinner make a solemn promise and firm resolve not to commit the same sin again.(Lev.5:5; Num.5:7) On the offenses to man besides confession to the person sinned upon there are penalties to be paid.(Lev. 5:1-20).

As in Isaiah 55:7, Repentance brings pardon and forgiveness of sin. The prophets and the apostles know of no other way of securing pardon other than repentance. Repentance then, qualifies a man for pardon, but it does not entitle him to it.

"Thank you Rabbi. Turning to the Greek Orthodox priest the moderator says, "What does the Greek Orthodox believe concerning repentance and sin Father?"

"Because, 'There is not a just man upon earth, that does good, and sins not. (Eccl.7:20; Num. 5:7) every mortal stands in need of this insistence on his "return" to God. In simplistic terms Hamartia is the Greek word for sin . . . means to miss the point. Metanoia is the Greek word for repentance, meaning to change perspective.

In other words, you repent by changing your perspective thereby eliminating the sin of incorrect choice in future situations.

The moderator now turns to the protestant Minister. Would you like to add anything to this subject Rev. Norman?"

"Yes, thank you. The doctrine of Repentance is very prominent in both the Old and New Testaments. What comes to mind is the touching of intellect which points to the previous subject matter you presented. It is Matt. 21:29—And he answered; I will not; but afterward he repented, and went. Here the word used for "repent" as in Greek means to change one's mind about a thing. This is well illustrated in the action of the Prodigal son.

In reference to emotions I would refer you to Cor.2. 7:9—Now I rejoice, not that ye were made sorry, but that you sorrowed to repentance; for ye were made sorry after a godly manner, that ye might receive damage by us in nothing. Also see Luke 10:13; Gen. 6:6. Here the Greek word for repentance in this way means "to be a care to one afterwards."

This certainly shows the mind (intellect) in tandem with feelings and emotions, which is perfectly in line with your diagram on the Brain-Mind-Soul and Spirit relationship.

By reflecting on the views of the various religions that have been expressed here, I think we can agree repentance occurs when one feels he or she has committed a wrong to God or some person. He or she seeks to gain forgiveness for the wrong. It begins with admission of guilt followed by a promise not to repeat the offense; in some cases restitution is made and in some way attempts to reverse the harm where possible.

Again we find major religions represented here all agree on an important and basic concept described in their definitions of Repentance and Sin.

One month later.

A MEETING ON RELIGIOUS UNDERSTANDING

Representatives for the original six religious beliefs are seated at the table. They represent the religious beliefs of Catholics, Protestants, Buddhists, Hindus, Judaist, and Islamists. This group represents about 4.5 billion people who believe in God.

The moderator calls the meeting to order.

"Gentlemen, I propose we call this gathering the first official meeting of "Religious understanding." If you agree please raise your hand." All hands go up.

"We all agreed after our last meeting to consider the material presented in the book "God is in your Molecules." Are there any questions?"

The chair recognizes Father Mc Cormack from our Catholic diocese.

"Mr. Chairman you claim we are all made of the same type of molecules but are nevertheless individual. If we all return to the earth as molecules we become part of the molecular make up of the world. Some molecules become food for animals and others nutrients for flora. Let us suppose an animal as a fox or a monkey eats molecules that were part of a human being, doesn't that imply that animal becomes part human?"

"Excellent observation Father. Let me explain it this way. Molecules are the building blocks of everything in the universe. Molecules unite with all types of matter, minerals, vegetation and the like. When a molecule unites with the molecules of a plant it becomes part of the plant. The rules of nature determine the molecule to become part of the host for growth.

If I may use a metaphor, let us look at the molecule as an automobile carrying its passenger to wherever directed.

After its use by one person someone else gets in the drivers seat and directs it to a new destination. No matter how many new drivers the auto has its only purpose is to provide transportation. That is the very nature of the molecule. Molecules have no, minds, brains or souls; they are a bit of the creative life source.

If we, in another way, look at the molecules as bricks we can understand their use to build bridges, buildings and the like. Bricks will eventually return to earth and break down to molecules that may become part of a vegetable that is eaten by a human being and become part of its growth pattern. This does not mean the human being is part brick.

Every molecule will eternally become part of the molecular structure of whatever unites with it. Molecular rotation is a life force that guarantees evolution."

The chair now recognizes the honorable Hindu monk.

The monk rises and asks, "What is the brain potential?"

The moderator replies, "Based on our present knowledge it could be centuries before that question can be answered.

Today we understand the brain has 100 billion neurons with each neuron having 7000 synaptic connections to other neurons.

A mind boggling statistic shows a brain of a three-year-old child has about 1 quadrillion synapses. This number declines with age, it stabilizes to 100 to500 trillion for an adult.

We only use a fraction our brain potential today and lose a great deal of our potential as we become adults. As time goes by we will have the ability to use most of our brain potential. The more neuron connections the greater potential we have to understand ourselves and the universe around us.

This new understanding and discovering will change our nature and bring us closer to the creator. Religion and science do complement one another.

May I quote from the Gospel of Mary Magdalene who quoted Jesus as saying, "All natures, all formed things, all creatures exist in and will again be resolved into their own roots, because the nature of matter is dissolved into the roots of its nature alone."

That beautiful statement to me reaffirms my belief that molecules, the roots, are that material that all nature is composed of; it travels from one type of matter to another."

The Buddhist monk stands and says, "In Buddhism it is believed the world is in a constant state of flux. This world is an illusion there is no permanence. What is your thought on that Mr. Moderator.

"I concur, molecules are in constant motion but we cannot see them, they are the material that illusions are made of. When a molecule leaves one form of matter (illusion) it becomes part of another matter (illusion) I see no conflict in your belief and mine. In fact Buddha said:

: "living beings after death are reborn and continue to exist. All living beings can become humans."

If we substitute the word "molecules" for "living beings" we can see that Buddha's thoughts are in line with the concept that molecules "living beings" never die and become part of any molecular structure including humans, plants or animals after leaving their present host."

A Lutheran minister comments that science is now experimenting in areas they should leave alone such as DNA.

The moderator replies; "I do not agree, let's look at science today. We see that there is most definitely an intelligent design in the universe. Some people are disturbed that science is going too far experimenting with DNA and neuron development. Recently a man lost the top of his thumb and agreed to have treatments to see if science could grow a new thumb. The experiment was successful and today he has full use of his thumb. Amazingly his new thumb has the identical fingerprint of the one he lost.

Present experiments are endeavoring to reconstruct neurons and build new sections of a damaged brain. Reconstructing body parts and neurons is giving better lives to people who have been suffering with maladies for years of their lives.

Intelligent design in the universe is being discovered every day and falls under universal laws that have always existed but not discovered previously. Science is proving the overall concepts that have been purported for years by prophets off all religions. We are all part of an intelligent design of the universe and as long as we use our discoveries to help mankind, we will survive.

It is logical to assume that evolution, over hundreds, perhaps thousands of years, will connect the dormant millions of neurons and synaptic connections in the human brain . . . These physical, chemical and electrical changes will provide us with the ability to discover additional universal laws that we can not even comprehend with today's brain.

As we know, nerve cells are known as neurons, located in the brain and spinal cord. They send and receive electro-chemical signals to and from the brain and nervous system. Did you know there are estimated to be over 100 billion neurons in our nervous system? In addition to this we have many more glial cells than neurons; they provide support functions for the neurons.

Research today is experimenting with regenerating damaged neurons. There is no religious agenda driving these experiments; researchers are just looking for the applicable universal law that applies. Reproducing an experiment that provides the same results is the scientific approach. No one is creating something unnatural; rather he or she is discovering what has always existed.

If we substitute the word "molecules" for "living beings" we can see that Buddha's thoughts are in line with the concept that molecules "living beings" never die and may become part of any molecular structure including plants or animals after leaving their present host.

Intelligent Design is the cement that binds religious beliefs and science. Prophets of major religions understood that. We as religious leaders are meeting today to point out the areas we agree on. We finally understand that we are all part of the same world and made of the same matter—molecules."

LOOKING AT SIMILAR BELIEFS.

Gentlemen, let's review some other ideologies and see how they confirm present thoughts on Intelligent design."

I ask our Hindu monk to begin."

"Thank you, Mr. Chairman, Hinduism goes back to 880 BC in India. A similar believe to yours is known as Jnana Marge, declaring, all things, men, animals, plants come from one thing or being to which they return.

Substitute the word "molecules," for the words "one thing" we have your theory of molecules being the basis for all life."

"Thank you that is a wonderful quote. It brings to mind a similar quote from Taoism (China) 604-531 BCE. Its founder Tao Te Ching wrote in his Treaty on the Tao and its power . . . all things come from non-being and return to non-being.

Substitute "molecules." for the words "non-being," and we have our molecular hypothesis.
In his day molecules were unknown so he used non-being.

Further proof is his statement, "Sages know, all things come from and blend into one and that they are themselves one with all things in the one."

Would the honorable Buddhist monk give us a similar quote from Zen?"

The monk replies, "Well Satori in Japan follows the key concept of Zen Buddhism, (5th-6th Cent.)."
"All phenomena are alike in their Buddha essence." That is in line with your molecular theory.
As we review these statements it becomes apparent they all are similar in their beliefs which go back cover thousands of years."

The Imam from Iran stands and is recognized by the chair.

I would like to comment on the oldest prophet from Persia.

We have reviewed concepts of major religions based on the interpretations and writings of scholars on old sacred manuscripts. The first religious ideology said to originate about 600 BCE by Iranian prophet Zarathustra.

The Greeks referred to him as Zoroaster but his countrymen of Iran knew him as the prophet Zarathustra. The cornerstone of his religion, known as Zoroastrianism is based on messages he received from the ancient supreme God called Ahuramazda. These revelations were interpreted by him in the form of 17 hymns his first scripture known as Gathas.

A library on various sacred texts, known as Avesta, written over a long period of time, gives interpretations of the 17 hymns of Zarathustra. It is noted that interpretations were difficult since they were made from the Gothic and Vedic languages.

Simply put the basis of the hymns condense to: "Think good thoughts, say good words and do good deeds."

This philosophy has been repeated and used by most religions including Christianity and Mohammadism. By the Christians in the Old Testament, Matthew 7:12: "Do unto others as you would have others do unto you."

Many of the religions we covered have used and agreed on concepts that have been advocated over thousands of years ago, from the old Persian empire. This certainly indicates that nothing is new."

The moderator stands, "That is an excellent way to end this meeting, God bless you all and good night."

MEETING ON MUSLIM AGNOSTIC

AND ATHEIST BELIEFS.

The moderator calls the meeting together and advises that all members in attendance will be called by their titles or beliefs, no names will be used. All discussions taking place will be absolutely unrecorded and not available for the press.

The moderator begins; "Our talks today as in the past are planned as a way to air and compare our beliefs and to see if we can live together without destroying each other.

Hopefully we will be able to understand why each person believes what he or she thinks is the right way and this will bring us together as one human to another."

'We have covered the view points of Atheists and Agnostics and will now start with any questions by Dr. X, who is an Atheist. Sir would you like to direct your questions to the Imam?"

"Thank you Mr. Moderator, I have some questions that are simple and direct for the Imam, here they are:

Do you believe Allah is the creator of the universe? The Imam nods his head.

Do you believe Allah created all living things? The Imam nods his head.

Do you believe every person will answer to Allah? The Imam nods his head.

Dr. X looks at the Imam and says, "You have agreed to all of the above questions, now we have a place to start.

It is my understanding that Muslims believe that every person outside of their faith is an infidel. Everyone in this room is an infidel and if we do not convert to Muslim beliefs we should be killed. This is stated in the Koran.

Is it not curious that Allah has created over five billion infidels, that if not converted, must be annihilated by a little more than one billion Muslims? This cannot be a mistake since Allah does not make mistakes and if anyone thinks so it is blasphemy. That person is condemned to death.

Muslim extremists tell us, do not follow the intent of the Koran. Their interpretations of the Koran suit their own desires. The infidel to them is any person not believing in what they say. They say these people are violating Allah's laws. This gives them the right to kill five billion infidels. It seems to me that these Muslims are correcting a mistake that Allah has made by creating so many infidels and so few Muslims. If so they are blasphemous and should be killed by other Muslims for doubting Allah's laws as described in the Koran.

For example in 2:191 . . . Kill the disbelievers wherever we find them. Or, perhaps, 9:5 . . . Fight and slay the pagans, seize them, beleaguer them, and lie in wait for them in every stratagem.

If I were not an atheist I would think that an all supreme Allah or creator would not need mortals to do his bidding. Allah would have created six billion Muslims, and there would be no problem."

The Agnostic interjects, "If I were to choose a religion I would not opt for a God that says kill infidels if they don't convert. Infidels from my understanding then could be your friends, neighbors or family members. My choice would be to go with the God who preaches "Love your enemies as yourself." Why would an all powerful God want to kill any of his children?" It seems to me these ideas are man made." Why have Muslims broken away from the teachings of Jesus when their religion looks up to him as a prophet as well as Adam, Moses, John the Baptist, and Noah who do not advocate that you should kill anyone who does not believe what they do?"

The Imam clears his throat and says, "I believe you gentlemen have a misconception of Muslim theology: There are many misquotations from the Koran but consider this, viii.12 says, "I will instill terror into the hearts of the Infidels, strike off their heads then, and strike off from them every fingertip." We must note that the first person narrative says "I will instill . . . ." This is God speaking it does not tell the Moslems to do it.

If we proceed to verse 61 you will find,—"But if the enemy incline towards peace, do you also incline towards peace and trust in God, for he is the one who hears and knows."

At that time Mohammed and his followers were attacked by tribes of pagans. Mohammad was enraged by these pagan practices of burying selected daughters alive. There were no Christians or Jews in that encounter.

So you see single lines should not be taken out of context unless you place it in the history of that moment.

The moderator concludes the meeting and says, "I hope we can meet again and clear up misconceptions that we all have about religious believes and the facts in history."

Every person is a miracle; you are the only one like you in the universe.

THEOLOGY vs. ATHEISM

Back in 1772, d Holbach said "All children are born atheists; they have no idea of God."

That statement cannot be proven or disproved.

One might add why aren't children born with the innate knowledge that God has set up a religion for him or her to abide by, and have faith in, determined by where he or she is born. Prior to the 18th century came the notion called theistic innatism that all people believe in God from birth. This cannot be proven or disproved.

There are "Strong" atheists and "Weak" atheists. Weak may include agnostics whereby strong absolutely affirm that God does not exist. There are also similar descriptions of negative and positive atheists. Atheists believe not to believe.

What is faith? Place your foot on the gas pedal, do you have faith the car will respond?

Do atheists and religious believers agree that we are all made up of molecules? We can't see them but we have faith they exist.

Is every child born an atheist? No. Then what makes some believe in a particular theology?

The "Essence of Energy" is the source of life. Neutrinos exist and can be proven.

Atheists can label this energy with a scientific explanation; believers call this energy the creative force or God. The creative energy cannot be seen but it's real to all. The theoretical atheist would say energy cannot be seen but that does not make it God. It is a force of nature that can be recognized and reproduced. Both agree energy cannot be seen with the naked eye but disagree on what to call it.

The faith based individual points to his theology which is based on prophets who have interpreted and determined, or stated, what and where God is and what he wants as written in the Bible, Torah or Quran.

The practical atheist has faith that what can be reproduced is reality. However, what can be reproduced in this world may not work on the moon or some other planet. His faith is perhaps limited by his environment and his present perception.

Some people are born with talents or understanding beyond what we might call average.

Some are born with mental or physical impairments. Some people blame God. But every soul is living out experiences dictated by universal laws at play.

There is no good or bad, however humans set up criterion for ethics and morality. For example:

THE SEVEN SINS

PRIDE: Hubris, smugness, complacency and undue high opinion of oneself.

Exaggerated self esteem of ones self.

SLOTH : Slowness, indolence, laziness and idleness.

ENVY: Feeling ill will because of another's advantages. Jealousy, backbiting, grudge, coveting and lust.

ANGER: Resentful or revengeful, a feeling of displeasure caused by an injury or mistreatment. Wrath, fury, animosity, hatred and outrage.

GREED/AVARICE: Excess, gluttony, (overeating) desires for more than one needs or deserves.

LUST: Excessive sexual desire, desire to gratify the senses. Bodily appetite, lechery.

GLUTTONY: Overindulgence, eating too much.

THE SEVEN VIRTUES

WISDOM: Based on ones knowledge, experience and understanding a sound course of action based on a quality of judging.

JUSTICE: Fair, right, truth, impartial, being or correct, reward or penalty as deserved.

TEMPERANCE: Self restraint in conduct and moderation in all things.

COURAGE: Facing anything and dealing with it when recognized as painful, difficult, or dangerous. (Having the courage of ones convictions.)

FAITH: Trust, an unquestioning belief (as in God) that does not require proof.

HOPE: Desire with expectation. Feeling what is wanted will happen.

LOVE: Tender feelings of affection. Devotion can be a strong passionate affection for someone. Love also is the acceptance and forgiving someone regardless of his or her beliefs or actions. In Christian theology (a). God's love for man; (b) spontaneous, altruistic love.

Every other living thing animal, vegetable or mineral survives under universal laws.

Have you ever heard of a dog, cat, ape or lion with an ethical or moral code? No.

Laws regarding ethics and morality are irrelevant to them. The same universal laws also apply to humans regardless of their moral and ethical beliefs. If a "good" or "bad' person jumps off the San Francisco bridge the universal laws of gravity determine their outcome.

A person makes choices throughout his or her life that dictates his or her future. When they select or make a choice contrary in universal law they lose.

When a person dies their molecular structure returns to the earth of this world. These molecules continue to live and are the substances that will support new life.

The soul moves on overseen by the Holy Spirit that is in us all.

Neutrinos . . . Can They Create Matter?
What would Atheists and Agnostics think?

If we an put atheist and an agnostic in our first fictitious scenario and gave them a pair of our nanotechnology glasses it is most likely they would agree that reality is what they saw, molecules. After all, every time they would put the glasses on they would see the same thing. This is the scientific method. The same type of molecules are in everyone, however, everyone is different when the glasses come off.

They may not concede an unknown force created those molecules but they must concede they see them. Faith enters the picture at this point; religious believers say that God created these molecules and everything else in the universe. The atheists say "prove it."

The question presents itself, why do we use about 10% of our brain capacity? Are we using more than humans did two hundred years ago? Why are some people born with extraordinary abilities in math and music?

It seems logical that our brain is in the process of evolution and that ultimately humans will use more of their brain capacity. Perhaps at that time we will have neuron connections that will give us the insight to better understand the transcendental nature of God.

For example, we have some autistic children who can play the classics on the piano with no training. Others astound us with their abilities to do advanced math with no training.

How is this possible? We know that certain areas of the brain control emotions, others physical functions. We can record brain activity by areas that virtually light up.

With today's advances in brain scanning we can see what part of the brain is activated.

It stands to reason that if we had ten times the neuron connections than we use today there is no telling what we could comprehend. How is this possible? There are studies going on today that scientifically prove that there are such things as neutrinos that pass through our bodies night and day and most of the time we are not affected by them.

However, if our molecules line up at the proper angle they act as a magnet and the neutrinos that are pouring through our cells unobstructed by its molecular matter can incredibly enter and become part the cell. Up to this point neutrinos have been passing through the cells without incident. The neutrino enters as energy and becomes part of the molecule. It converts the cells mass changing the cells composition. The result is increased matter in the person's molecular structure.

This certainly could be one way energy from the outside world can convert to matter and make real changes in our actions and thinking, perhaps by creating new connections in our neuron brain matter giving us a greater ability to think and comprehend more than we do today. So, there is a scientific way of connecting our neurons. Religious groups will say this is God at work. Atheists will say it's the science of adapting to new sources of energy.

Science will settle this dispute over future centuries. When everything can be proven scientifically, science and religion will blend. Our problem today is that we are not equipped to understand the "essence of energy," the creator. We are limited by our own molecular make-up. We are not equipped to think in terms of a transcendental force that is beyond our capacity to understand. To the writer, this is proof of God. No one is asked to fly that has no wings. We will receive all knowledge when we have earned it. Do he best we know how, decisions we make now will determine our future.

THE AUTHORS OWN COMMENTS CONTINUE
BEYOND THE UNIFIED FIELD THEORY

Premise one: the universe is structured under a unified field that determines all reactions in the universe. This is a system of natural law that polices all actions in the universe.

The explosion of stars, the formulating of new galaxies and planets all conform to the "rules" of the universe. The creator has designed these rules and they are unchangeable.

For example, man has devised an atomic and hydrogen bomb that has the capability to change the molecular nature of the atmosphere it contacts on explosion. Atoms have been centrifuged to become ions by throwing off electrons from their orbits. This destruction of the atomic natural state is not in the natural order of the universe. It may take years or centuries but eventually the natural order of the universe prevails and the areas of the atomic impact are neutralized by the atoms with missing electrons, taking on new electrons that take them from the ion state [incomplete] to their natural state containing the proper number of electrons. [Their complete state] So even though man may change the structure of atoms temporarily, they will return to their original state under a set of universal laws of nature where time is meaningless.

Premise two: there are no new structures in the universe. There are changes in form as from solids to gases. The uniting of atoms to create molecules and thus different forms of matter lies within the rules structuring the universe.

Premise three: Atoms can neither be made nor destroyed. Atoms in the universe today are no different than those atoms from the beginning of time. Everything in the universe "is" and will "always be." We discover new ways of tapping into what "is" but we do not make or create things. We keep making new discoveries only to find out new discoveries make them obsolete. Sending radio waves or signals around the world was no different 2000 years ago than it is today. If we could travel back in time we could send TV signals and radio messages anywhere in the ancient world. But, man at that time had not discovered how to transmit and pick up signals through the atmosphere. The point being, natural laws then were the same as they are in the year 2005.

Premise four: Every atom is an available brick to support a life force.

Premise five: Natural birth of a child begins when the man's sperm unites with the woman's egg, or ovum. The molecular nature by the way of DNA or genetic history of the male's sperm unites with the DNA and genetic history of the female's egg. A new molecular structure is formed which is unlike the father or mother. This new baby has its own DNA extracted from both father and mother. In other words, the whole {new child} is not equal to the sum of its parts. It is more than the sum of its parts.

To follow this theory, the new being has the potential to grow physically and spiritually. The fetus is fed new molecular structure via the umbilical tube. After birth the molecular structure from the mother's milk is the nutrition that provides for the babies growth. After weaning the child eats and drinks food as the parents, which of course is also molecular nutrition.

Every atom has a physical nature that can support life. The birth of a child as we know it is actually the formation of a new molecular structure with the physical and spiritual potential to grow.

Material life was formed when the creator created the atom. The spirit of the creator is in every atom. Therefore life does not start at conception or when the egg and sperm unite. Those are instances of making molecular changes.

POLITICS AND RELIGION

Politics is one's opinion on political matters: described sometimes as the science or art in government. In the USA it is predominately the republicans versus the democrats, both parties take every opportunity to knock the other party. Each party is backed by religious groups of varying opinions.

Can either party claim that God is a republican or a democrat? How ridiculous, but each party asks God to take their side.

IS GOD PARTIAL TO ANY RELIGION?

Ask yourself; is God, Allah, Yahveh [YHVH] or the Lord, partial to any religious belief?

Is the creator a Muslim, Catholic, Protestant, Jew or Buddhist? Religious beliefs are based on memories centuries old and conveyed as history then transformed by scholars into religious beliefs and dogma . . . described as an arrogant assertion of opinion. Wars, the Crusades as an example, over a thousand years ago, were fought with opposite sides declaring God was on their side.

All religions are from man's idea and thoughts of the creator's laws. They are mans attempt to explain the unexplainable.

SCIENCE AND RELIGION

With an understanding of the above we come to the realization that science does not oppose religious beliefs, it in fact supports them. We get lost in the semantics. We are all part of the Creator. Our molecular structure is what the universe is made of. Our color, race, and ethnicity, as well our beliefs and opinions, no matter how scholarly, will not change that fact. Every molecule is unique and each as important as the other.

REVIEWING RELIGIOUS DOCTRINES

ANCIENT WORSHIP

Motivation for worship: Humans need to feel comfortable with other humans in the universe, for man does not live alone, it is important to have workable relations with other humans. Man cannot control nature and society, so he searches for harmony with those he lives with while continually searching for the original force of the universe.

Primitives—people who live close to nature and are isolated from highly technical and cultural societies. Australian aborigines, pygmies of Africa, and scattered jungle tribes throughout the world are good examples.

Today cultural, educational and technological changes are taking place in many of these areas with exposure of modern man, but traditions die hard. Individuals still cling to role playing since their customs have been made sacred by their ancestors and by divine powers. The chief cause of religions and magical rituals has not changed for thousands of years. Individuals seek reassurances and favorable outcomes for their lives.

Today the world still has sacred places of graves, trees and fetishes.[the magic in inanimate objects].Even taboos exist in places like Haiti, where a taboo on a person or place or action are sacred because they have the power to cause good or evil.

The veneration of many powers and spirits are traced to primitive people who venerated stones, plants and animals, and statues of Gods. They are said to be full of Mana, an indwelling of power that can cause a kind of extraordinary action.

Finally, primitive peoples believe in a great God up in the sky, who made everything, gods, men and animals. He is the ultimate law lawgiver and overseer. This God is beyond magic and cannot be reached through prayer.

FOUR BASIC MAGIC'S

When in fear of danger or bad consequences magic is performed to get favorable results.

1   Preventative magic: Wards off undesired happenings.
2   Productive magic : Brings about happenings
3   Sympathetic magic: Presumes like produces like—certain parts of the body
     return sympathy with the organ to which they once belonged.
4   Black magic: Seeks to harm, has roots in sympathetic magic, as making an
     image of wax of an enemy then piercing it in the heart with a pin, killing the
     enemy.

Fetishism: We should note that Shamans use powers of inanimate objects such as distinctive stones or animal horns. Shamans are also said to be able to guide souls after death into the next world.

Common and primitive people in the world abound with beliefs that ills are caused by powers and spirits found in every natural object, beast, plant and human being. Magic, sacrifices and prayer are preventative actions to divine these powers to do good; but this is only achieved by constant vigilance and care. Their best course of action is to always follow traditional procedures without deviation. They are born into these beliefs and brought up following them via their parents. Head hunting and eating parts of your enemies' dead body for power are examples, as is the adoration of monkeys in some parts of India, expressing the idea they could be your relatives.

Death is viewed as a departure of a soul from its body, which it has directed during its lifetime. Disembodied souls are regarded with fear and must be placated. These are souls that met with violent deaths. It is essential to give proper ceremonies for these souls or they may become demonic. Some Pagan beliefs have been carried over into the contemporary religious beliefs of the twentieth century.

POST EXILE OF JUDAISM . . . 539 BC. To 70 AD

The Hebrew nation was destroyed by the Babylonians in 597 BC. Rebellion broke out in Judah 606 BC. Nebuchadnezzar returned and destroyed everything; the land lay in ruins for 150 years. At this time the Hebrew religion seemed to have disappeared. But the Jews [a term derived from Judeans] remained after the Hebrew nation was destroyed.

Two prophets, Ezekiel and Isaiah, appear to prepare for the return to their homeland. Ezekiel restores temple rights. Isaiah sees the day when the Jewish faith, purified, would become the whole world's way of life.

A new class of teachers and Rabbis expound the law of the prophets. Judaism a new clear-cut legalistic religion was born. This was a way of life established in laws and ritual, which was laid on the Jewish conscious. These ways were derived from many people including Greeks, Romans, Philistines, Egyptians and many others.

Hebrews was a term derived from Hibre, applied by Egyptians and Mesopotamanians about 1500 BC. to the Semitic wanderers who were called

"Desert Raiders"or'Boundary crossers." In Palestine one group of these people called themselves "Children of Israel" claiming decent from the twelve sons of Israel. Jacob, whose father was Isaac and Grandfather Abraham, In Palestine, they were joined by non-Israelites, Hebrews who in time adopted their national identity and faith. Why do Palestinians think that Jews shouldn't be in Palestine? Jews lived there thousands of years ago.

THE QUABBALA, THE SECRET
DOCTRINE OF ISRAEL

Hebrew theology was divided into three distinct parts, as follows:

The Law—all the children of Israel were taught The Law.

The Soul of the Law—the Mishna, revealed only to the teachers and Rabbins. The Soul of the Soul of the Law, the Quabbala, teachings were concealed and only the highest initiates of the Jews were instructed in its secret principals.

According to certain Jews, Moses ascended Mt. Sinai three times, remaining in the presence of God forty days each time. In the first forty days the tales of the written law were delivered to Moses; he received The Soul of the Law the second forty days; during the last forty days God instructed him in the mysteries of the Quabbala, the Soul of the Soul of the Law.

Moses is said to have concealed in the first four books of the Pentateuch, the secret instructions he received from God, and for century's students of the Quabbala have sought therein the secret doctrine of Israel. As man's spiritual nature is concealed in his physical body so the unwritten law, the Mishna and the Quabbala is concealed within the teachings of the Mosaic Code. Quabbala means the secret or hidden tradition of the unwritten law.

According to an early Rabbi it was delivered to man in order that he might learn to understand the mystery of the universe about him and the universe within him. To the writer this seems to point to the fact that science is disclosing these secrets. Molecules are without us and are within us.

Christian D. Ginsburg has written from Adam it passed over to Noah, then to Abraham who immigrated to Egypt where he let a portion of the doctrine seep out. This was the way Egyptians obtained some knowledge of it and then other Eastern nations introduced it into their philosophical systems.

Moses initiated the seventy Elders in the Secret Doctrine and they transmitted it then from hand to hand. David and Solomon were the most initiated of all those initiates. Drawing from the unwritten secrets of earlier Jewish mysteries.

The simple Quabbalism of the first centuries of the Christian era gradually became an elaborate theological system, so involved that it was next to impossible to comprehend its dogma. Alchemy, Hermeticism, Rosicrucianism and Freemasonry are inextricably woven with the theories of Quabbalism.

A Synopsis of major Religions

SCIENCE ILLUSTRATED IN THE BOOK OF GENESIS

THE PROPHET MOSES

History has recorded Moses as the folk hero who led and rescued the Israelites from Egyptian slavery. He is said to have written the first five books of the Bible, Genesis, Exodus, Leviticus, Numbers and Deuteronomy in The Old Testament. There are thirty-nine books in the Old Testament. Many modern scholars feel the first five books came from many sources, who edited them carefully before they became the first five books of the Bible and eventually "Mosaic Law."

A set of laws developed slowly over centuries after Moses. Theses laws were not given directly to Moses. In the Jewish religion these laws are termed the "Mosaic Law" or "The Law," or in Hebrew "The Torah." In Greek, the first five books are called 'Pentateuch." The first book "Genesis means, coming into being. The Greeks were the first to translate the Bible in the 3rd century B.C. based on the works of seventy learned scholars.

It is interesting to note that in Hebrew God is "Elohim" which is plural for "Gods"

Genesis 3:22—Behold the man has become one of us, to know good and evil—

Genesis 11:7—Go to, let us go down, and there confound their language—Polytheism goes back in history, whereas Monotheism was a late development in the history of ideas. Monotheistic beliefs would have preferred not to use this plural term but it was so embedded in the religion it was left alone.

The Hebrew word "Lord" in English is YHVH mistakenly called "Jehovah". Modern scholars feel "Yahveh" [YHVH] is more accurate to "Lord." In general terms the word god was used for any deity whereas "God" expresses the one deity of the Bible.

Genesis 2:7—And the Lord God formed man of the dust of the ground, and breathed into his nostrils the breath of life; and man became a living soul. Is this not the same as molecules being rearranged to form molecules of a different formation—the human being? Is this not God's universal law that we term science today? Is this not an illustration of the compatibility of science and religion? Man was formed by what was already in existence—dust of the ground.

Note: Adam in Hebrew is individual man. Adam is also akin to mankind.

HINDUISM

Hinduism is over thirty centuries old. It is said that it started when light skinned Europeans invaded India via the Khyber Pass about 1500 BC and the dark skinned people they conquered, who were the creators of the Indus culture of central and western India. They brought with them Gods, as Shiva, God of reproduction, as well as the concept of re-incarnation and the Law of Karma.

The Indian culture was designed after the four oral scriptures of Hinduism. In 800 BC written literature appeared in Sanskrit the classical language of India. At this time Varne was introduced which was the cast system. Eventually 2000 subcastes appeared and dictated things like, different diets, no intermingling; no sleeping together, no intermarriage, no eating

    Kshatryias- - - warriors

    Vaishyas- - - artisans and peasants

    Shudras- - - servants

together every Sect had its own laws.

Titles were bestowed; Brahmins priests

"The Way of the Works" or [Karma Marga] Governs household life from prayers to Gods when working, to prayers to different Gods on retiring.

Darhma—requires visits to temples and going on pilgrimages to foreign places. The law of Karma determines whether one rises or falls in the scale of existence. If evil is done in this life you fall to a lower level even to animal or insect level and you could go to hell. To follow the Way of the Works is one of three ways to salvation.

The Way of Knowledge—Jnana Marga—more difficult than the way of the works. After 800 BC new rituals were brought about. All things men, animals, plants, come from one thing or being to which they return. [Here again science has established grounds for this thinking of 800 BC. We come from a molecular structure of the universe and return to it after death in a molecular form.]

Brahman—the highest aim here is to become an arhat, an enlightened monk intent on getting himself to Nirvana. In Rangoon and Bangkok there are temples of gold plated Buddha's. You may pray to the Buddha's but prayers cannot reach him since he is in Nirvana. Although it is meritorious to give gifts to Buddha, these gifts are given to the Sangha in order that he may be re-born as a monk. The monk compassionately instructs the layman in the right path.

Many Hindus today recognize three gods; Brahma, the creator; Vishnu the caretaker of the universe and Shiva the god of death or the destroyer.

BUDDHISM

The founder of Buddhism was born about 560 BC in India into the Kahatriya caste destined to be a ruling prince. In his late twenties he left his parents, wife and son to seek entrance to Nirvana. He could not find enlightenment from following the Brahmin beliefs so he turned to extreme asceticism of Mahavira for five years and found it debilitating. One day he sat under the Bo tree [from bodhi, or enlightenment, tree]. At a place that was renamed for him, as Budhgaya [the place of the enlightenment]. He wondered what created human misery. The answer came to him; it was desire, thirst, passion and wanting what was not possessed.

From this beginning came the Buddhist ethical code that all any constituents of living persons and the entire living world are in a constant state of flux. Nothing remains immune to change but Nirvana. All in this world is an illusion there is no permanence. This certainly would agree with intelligent design and the fact that we are all made up of a molecular nature that is constantly changing.

MAHAYANA BUDDHISM

ZEN

Zen in Japan is known as Ch'an in China, both are Dhyana. Zen tries to shock the seeker by presenting him with logical paradoxes [Koans] that will cause him to give up logical explanations and wait for intuition of his own Buddha essence.

One must seek flashes of insight and reject systematic study and discussions. This is known as Satori in Japan. The oneness of the universal self is pre-supposed. All phenomena are alike in their Buddha essence. Here again we reveal science at work. All things in the universe are composed of the same molecular materials in different arrangements, making them the same but unique but different from each other.

Mahayana Buddhism—Maya means great. Yana means vehicle—this is the Buddhism of Korea, Japan, China, Mongolia and Tibet where it is known as the "Great Ferry".

Whence did the Gautama Buddha come? He must have come from the heavens, come out of compassion for suffering mankind to be born from a woman. Here again the supposition that Buddha came from a woman conforms to the science that all forms in creation including man, must source from the molecular laws of the universe. Magic is not used or considered, there is no waving of a wand. Universal law has been established by the creator and all things comply with it.

There are numerous Mahayana Sects. The Pure Land sects, The Knowledge Sects, The Intuition Sects, The Mystery or True World Sects, The Vayrayana of Tibet and many others. Attempts are being made today to unify Buddhist Sects. This unification is an effort to convert all non-Buddhists in the world.

ZOROASTRIANISM

About the 7TH century BC in Iran its only prophet Zoroaster tried to reform the religion of his people. Mostly because it was priest ridden and demanded animal sacrifices. He is said to have trances where the wise Lord creator of all heaven and earth gave him messages in the form of hymns. These hymns became the first scriptures of Zoroastrianism called the Gathas. God and the devil convulse the world—God will win—Final punishment will come to the devil and all those who follow him.

JAINISM [INDIA]

In the sixth century BC presumed the life and teachings of Mahavira. Today there are over two million followers, mostly in Bombay area. He rejected Vedas, a heresy, the sacrificial system of priests, and of the caste system. This religion rejected monistic Brahmanism on philosophical grounds.

Mahavira is purported to have said, "A man is not saved by God or priests but by his own efforts." He did say, "Man, you are your own friend; why do you wish for a friend beyond yourself?"

He achieved moksha [salvation] by severe asceticism. He never injured any living thing because of the soul in it, a practice called ahimsa [nonviolence].

TAOISM

One of the two major religions in China, it is rooted in Confucianism, the practice of ancient China. Basically, that all things and all natural processes were the interaction between masculine [Yang] positive energy mode and the Yin a feminine passive mode. Yin is at rest. Whereas, day, air, sun etc, are Yang. [Active].

The principal of law and order was called the Tao [the way] all was well when one conformed within this law. Demons, devils, and dangerous spirits are rebellious to the Tao.

Tao-Te-Ching wrote a treatise called, "Treatise on the Tao and its power." It says that all things come from nonbeing and return to nonbeing. Isn't this the same concept today? All things come from unseen molecular beings and return to unseen molecular beings upon dying? This is science verifying ancient old beliefs.

It continues, the Sages know all things come from and blend into one and that they are themselves one with all things in the one. Again science agrees and confirms, in today's terms the universe is composed of untold trillions of molecules making the whole, some molecules come from the whole as human beings, some as animals, some as plants but all blend back into the universal whole because they never left.

The philosophy continues regarding human actions. People would get along if they were non-meddlesome and behave with instinctive spontaneity. When they respond in "The Way" the results are love, goodness, sincerity, and they enjoy a long healthy life.

TAOISIM AS MAGIC

Early Taoist searched for long life by eating things like gold. They used the alchemist furnace in order to make gold eatable. They advised a way of life away from cities and organized civil life.

CONFUCIANISM

Confucius Kung fu-Tzu born in 531 BC. He was fatherless at three years old. His devoted mother gave him aristocratic training and he aspired to government office. After his mother died he turned his home into a private school where he taught the six disciplines that he was trained in. namely, history, poetry, manners, government, divination and music. He broke tradition by bringing in poor boys. He taught Shu; do as one would be done by. Found today in the Christian's golden rule, "Do unto others as you would have others do unto you." He felt he was designated by heaven to teach his doctrines of mutuality {Shu}.

After his death his followers used his teachings and they became known as the "Five Classics".

CHRISTIANITY

Christians regard Jesus as an incarnation of God the Father and therefore the source of primary revelation. Christianity emerged from Judaism but over the centuries has absorbed some doctrinal and cultic elements form the Greeks and Romans. Jesus was born in 4 or 6 BC in Bethlehem of Judea, and grew up in Nazareth of Galilee. This was a time of Jewish rivalries and great penetration of Greek and Roman culture. Jesus was ten years old when the Zealots of Galilee were uprising at which time he must have witnessed their bloody suppression. At thirty years old Jesus went down to the Jordan River to hear John the Baptist and was baptized by him. During his immersion Jesus experiences a call to prophecy. After a period of solitary preparation he appeared in Galilee proclaiming that the Kingdom of Heaven was at hand. He recruited twelve disciples to accompany him while he taught in synagogues and to large crowds in the countryside. He claimed that first importance must be given to justice, love and mercy issuing from the inner self. He said, "Men of old were told an eye for an eye, but I say to you love your enemy." His preaching's were addressed to the plain people and he was known for his parables. Miracles of healing accompanied his ministry. During the Passover of 28 AD he was seized in Jerusalem, accused before Pilate the Roman procurator, and crucified on Mt. Calvary along with two criminals. The disciples dispersed.

THE APOSTOLIC AGE

A few weeks later at Pentecost the disciples met in an upper room in Jerusalem and experienced the descent of the Holy Spirit. They were then empowered to spread the Gospel throughout the world. Jewish authorities prohibited the disciples to teach the new faith in their synagogues or anywhere else and charged them to teach only the Torah. Stephen, one of them, was seized and stoned to death.

An ardent Pharisee, Paul, was active in seeking suppression of the Christians, but on his travel to Damascus to pursue this cause, he had a blinding vision and heard the voice of Jesus. Converted to the Christian faith he became a leader in missionary works among the Gentiles.

Paul was sent to Rome and was imprisoned there and became a Christian martyr. Christian's first meetings took place in homes but then built their own churches. A new scripture was needed for these churches. Four gospels were written. The letters of Paul, Peter, James and John were given scriptural rank. The four gospels were written, Mark, Mathew, Luke and John, to them were added Luke's, Acts of the Apostles. These works were gathered into the canon of the New Testament [ultimately totaling twenty seven books] to accompany the use of the Jewish scriptures of the Old Testament, [thirty nine books].

ISLAM

Islam is rooted in three religions, Zoroastrianism, Judaism, and Christianity. Islam means 'submission' and its adherents are Muslims [Moslems]—submitters to Allah, [God]. Its unique character comes from its Arabic origins.

MUHAMMAD [OR MOHAMMED]

Mohammad was born in Mecca about 570 A.D. and was an orphan at six. He became a ward of his grandfather and then of his uncle Abu Talib. Growing up he took a disapproving view of Arabian polytheism and social disunity. At twenty-five he married his wealthy employer, a widow and had leisure time to reflect and brood on religious problems. He wondered, after looking at Christianity and Judaism, why no prophet had yet come to Arabians to prepare them for the Last Judgment.

At forty years of age he began to have ecstatic experiences of conversations with the Angel Gabriel from whom he received revelations from Allah. He was astonished to find he was the needed prophet to Arabia. He was rejected in his own town so when his wife, Khadijah and his uncle Abu Talib both died about the same time, he felt a loss of their protection so he left for Tathrib on a hijra [hewgira] "withdrawal." He was invited there by some of his followers in 622 AD from which all Muslim dates are reckoned. He became the civil and religious leader and the town was renamed for him to Medina a Nabi ["the city of the prophet"] In 631 AD he took the Meccan's city making it and its central shrine, the Kabah, the holy center for Muslim pilgrimage. Mohammad died of a fever the year following his takeover of Mecca. Shortly after Mohammad's death his revelations were gathered into the Quran. His friend and father in law, Abu Bakr became his successor [caliph]. Mohammad's recorded religious duties yielded the "Five Pillars." The consolidation and expansion had begun and spread to Syria, Palestine and later to Persia, India and beyond the Himalayas.

MUSLIM BELIEFS

1   Allah is the one true God and does not share his divinity with any associate.
2   Angels surround Allah's throne, Gabriel having the highest rank. The fallen Angel Shaitin who with his demons is busy leading men astray.
3   There are four scriptures, the Torah of Moses, the Zabur [Psalms] of David. The Evangel of Jesus and the revelations of Muhammad, compiled after his death into the Quran or Koran. The last corrects and gives final form to the truth of the others.
4   Allah's human messengers are the prophets, being Mohammad, Adam, Noah, Abraham, Moses, and Jesus. He denied that Jesus was crucified in his own person. He held however that Jesus was virgin born, performed miracles and ascended into heaven. He was incensed by the doctrine that Jesus was the Son of God. A last day is coming.

Much attention was given to elevate the morals of his followers, as prohibiting gambling and wine. He raised the status of women by giving them property rights and disallowing divorce from them without providing for their economic needs. Arabian tribal organization with its blood violence and vengeance was to be transformed into a means of expressing inclusive brotherhood and respect for human rights. Tribal feuds were substituted with the Holy war [Jihad] to be made on nonbelievers if the latter provided provocation.

THE FIVE PILLARS

Shortly after Mohammad's death his revelations were gathered into the Quran. His prescription concerning religious duties yielded what is called The Five Pillars.

1   Repetition of the Shahadah or creed: "There is no God but Allah and Muhammad is the prophet of Allah."

2   Prayer [Salat] at Friday the mosque and five times a day facing Mecca.

3   Alms [Zakat] for the needy.

4   Fasting during the month of Ramadan from dawn to dusk.

5   Pilgrimage [hajj] a least once in a lifetime to Mecca, either in person or by proxy. In addition, orthodox practice requires women to go veiled in public, but men were to mingle freely without racial or class discrimination.

There are many Muslim diversifications but there are three traditional groups:

A.   The Sunnis who follow the Quran.

B.   The Shiites [or partisans of Allah] who view the son-in-law of Mohammad and his descendants as the only legitimate Imams [divinely designated leaders].

C.   The Sufis or mystics who overlap with the Sunnis but feel they have the possibility of mystical communication directly with Allah.

Recent developments: A dichotomy has developed since Muslims on the one hand appropriate western science and technology and on the other hand set up defenses against western religion and culture.

There has been and remains a violent reaction against Israel on what is regarded as Muslim soil.1

Finally, The Fruit of Islam, commonly known as black Muslims, want the rigid separation of the races and demand a section of the United States to be carved out to them and given as reparations for the enforced slavery of Negroes in the past. However, orthodox Muslim leaders reject this movement's claim and charge it with distorting Mohammad's teachings. The story is told of Muhammad that the Angel Gabriel with seventy wings came to him as a toddler. He cut open the child, withdrew the heart. Gabriel then cleansed the heart of the black drop of original sin [in every human being] then replaced it.2

1 The Worlds Religions by John B. Noss. "The Secret Teachings of all Ages"—"The Faith of Islam" by Manly Palmer Hall.

THE ANCIENT CATHOLIC CHURCH

[150-1054 AD] The Catholic Church gained its name from its claim to be catholic or universal. The Catholic Church has many struggles from opposition without and heresy from within its church. In the fourth century Christianity triumphed with the accession of Constantine to the throne. By the end of the century it was the Imperial state church. The Popes claimed that since St. Peter was the first apostle of the church he founded, he should be accorded primacy among the churches. The pressing of this claim brought about the division of the church between the Roman west and the Orthodox east.

SHINTO

Shinto—"The religion of the Gods" is strictly Japanese. Its belief is that all Japanese are the descendants of the Gods, called Kawi. Japan is the land of the Gods.

THE MEDIEVAL CHURCH

[1054-1517] During the middle ages 1204 came the sack of Constantinople and its capture in AD 1453 by the Turks, deepening the separation of east and west. In the Greek speaking areas of the Roman Empire the Eastern churches spread southward into Egypt and then northward into Balkans and Russia. Many congregations boasted that they were founded by an Apostle and therefore they had equal claims of venerability contrary to the supremacy claims by the Bishop of Rome. They differ and continue to differ with the west on many matters as baptism, celibacy and many other issues.

In the west, the Papacy attained its greatest secular power in the 11th to 13th centuries to the degree that Pope Gregory VII forced the German Emperor to plead for Papal clemency by standing barefoot in the snow at Canossa. Universities were founded and in them scholasticism devoted itself to exploring and corroborating the dogmas of the Church. The greatest of the scholars was St. Thomas of Aquinas who produced the Summa Theologica adapting Aristotle's methods to Christian revelation that is still honored as authoritative by Catholics today.

SIKHISM

One of the youngest religions founded in the 16th century. Nanak, from Hindu parents had a vision in the forest of one God whose name is true. He thought if everyone used this name, Muslims and Hindus' would become Sikhs, [disciples]. Thus there would be no need for Allah, Brahma, Vishnu or Shiva. He did away with the Hindu taboo of not eating meat, saying God ordained man to be served by lower creatures. He accepted Karma and the law of re-incarnation. "True name" pre-destined all creatures, clearly a Muslim teaching. His religion merged Hindu and Muslim beliefs.

THE PROTESTANT REFORMATION AND ITS
CATHOLIC COUNTERPART

[1517-1700]. A new individualism arose with commercial towns independent of feudal barons, a new demand came about for freedom and reform. The common man wanted the Bible in his own language. In Germany, Martin Luther [1483-1546] was convinced the scriptures of the Church had succumbed to unchristian pomp, worldliness and pride and had resorted to unscriptural devices for gain. In 1517 in protest, he nailed his 95 Thesis to the door at Wittenberg and precipitated the Protestant Reformation. Simply stated, that every Christian through faith can enjoy God's favor without the necessary mediation of Priest or Pope. The true Church are the people who have surrendered themselves through inward change to Christ and find there, ultimate authority, not in the Pope but in the Bible made understandable by the Holy Spirit through faith.

The Church of England, through Henry VIII, established the Reformation in England. The non-conformist Puritans carried the Protestant cause to New England in their pursuit of full liberty of conscience.

The Catholics started a Counter Reformation in The Council of Trent, which met over 18 years [1545-1563] where they instituted reforms in church discipline and management and redefined the Catholic theological position. The result was a new spirit and zeal bringing about new orders such as the most famous "Jesuit Order," founded by Ignatius Loyola [1491-1566].

THE CHURCH IN THE MODERN WORLD

[1700 on] The 18th century Deism cooled the religious ardor of the time for the Church of England but witnessed John Wesley and associates bring the Methodist Church to the America's. This movement strove to restore through "conversion" the sense of immediacy in God's presence in human lives. This movement of missionaries began in the 18th century and intensified through the 19th century, not only in America but Europe and every part of the world. Christian education programs expanded through the 20th century. The conflict between science and religion broke out which led to Fundamentalism of the 20th century. This change brought about the World Council of Churches. There was a need for churches to unite in a post-Protestant and post-Christian era to create a new unity and effectiveness for their religious strength.

The Catholic Church in 1854 proclaimed the Immaculate Conception of the Virgin Mary, and then in 1870 declared the doctrine of papal infallibility. The dogma, the assumption of the uncorrupted body of the Virgin Mary to heaven after her death, was proclaimed in 1950. These were attempts to harden doctrine into set positions unalterable. Liberalism was alive and showed up when Pope John XXIII in 1959 summoned an Ecumenical Council embracing the entire Catholic world. Several sessions were held in the 1960's, attended by 2500 Cardinals and Bishops. Even official+ observers from the Protestant faith were given a place. A declaration declared that Jews were not to be held peculiarly responsible for the death of Christ. Bishops were also given a greater voice in the management of the church.

Christ's teachings were reaffirmed in the 20th century when Christians, both Catholic and Protestant actively joined the Negro civil rights movement in the1960s.

QUESTIONS TO PONDER

Of all the religions highlighted in this text what was the common reason for their creation.

How many of the religions in this text aim at having everyone in the world as believers in their ideology?

How many believe all non-believers should perish?

How many of these same religions started with a prophet who received instructions from God?

How many of these religions set up ethical and moral boundaries for their believers?

How many of the above groups believe in a Heaven or Nirvana after death?

How many believe that science works with religious beliefs?

Why is one prophet more credible than another?

How many prophets were mortal?

How many prophets were married?

How many prophets had children?

How many prophets claim they spoke directly to God?

How many prophets claim they spoke through Gods intermediary?

How many religions have been affected by political or governmental leaders?

Why are your religious beliefs more valid than someone else's beliefs?

Can you live in peace with people of another religious persuasion?

Do you believe God is exclusive to your religious beliefs?

Do you see intelligent design as a positive force in your religious beliefs? Why?

THE KEY TO SURVIVAL

Adaptation in a world structured by intelligent design is the key to change and survival. All matter is composed of molecular combinations. The atoms of these molecules are the same. When arranged in different configurations they appear differently, molecules that make wood are the same, we see them as boards for building materials, baseball bats, furniture and many other configurations. Hydrogen molecules are the same, combined with other molecules they become part of a new form but when that form is broken down into molecular structures they are still hydrogen molecules. Intelligent design in the universe as we know it is composed of these molecular structures. We as human beings are made up of combinations of theses molecules. They are a part of us from birth to physical death. After death of animal, or vegetable or flora, molecules remain in the universe and assimilate into new forms. They can become a part of animal, mineral or vegetable or liquid, compounding with other molecules. The point being, there is no death for molecules there is transformation and molecular adaptation to the environment.

Natural selections then follow intelligent design . . . Absolute universal formulas are at play. Changes come about when responses follow a pre-set formula for change. We are a bundle of intricate systems of neurons that formulate functional needs as genetic, biochemical and physiological and balance them off with evolutionary or instinctual adaptations. If we choose the correct adaptation, we live and contribute to our species. Survival and future discoveries are made possible by the new construction of adaptive neurons not previously available for making choices. It seems to the writer that the molecular nature of the universe is the science, by intelligent design, which set the tracts for what can or cannot be done according to pre-set universal formulas. However, the esoteric nature of man is his spiritual essence which is unique to every human being. Different religions express the spirit or soul in their own way. Religious ideologies do not increase their membership by showing proof on why they are correct, rather they ask for faith that what they say is true.

Adaptation is the key to change and survival in our world. All matter is composed of molecular combinations. The atoms of these molecules are the same. When arranged in different configurations they appear differently. Molecules that make wood are the same, we see them as boards for building materials, baseball bats, furniture and many other configurations. Regardless of how we see them broken down they are the same molecular structures.

Hydrogen molecules are the same, combined with other molecules they become part of a new form but when that form is broken down into molecular structures they are still hydrogen molecules.

The universe as we know it is composed of the same molecular structures. We as human beings are made up of combinations of theses molecules. They are part of us from birth to death. After death of animal, or vegetable or flora, molecules remain in the universe and are assimilated into new forms. They can become part of animal, mineral or vegetable or water, compounding with other molecules. The point being, there is no death for molecules there is transformation and molecular adaptation to the environment. The laws of the creator are unchangeable. When we adapt to our environment we understand these laws and we grow. If we do not adapt we leave this material universe.

Nature is structured under the universal laws of adaptability. For example the Blue headed wrasse fish is capable of being male or female. These fish are said to move in social groups of many females and one male. If the male dies the largest female changes to the male sex and the species survives. Another sea creature known as the Sea squirt in the early stages of its life falls to the bottom of the sea looking for a rock to attach to. It feeds on most of its own brain material since it does not need a brain to survive just food.

Today, Evolutionary psychologists say natural selection is a feedback process that chooses among alternative designs on the basis of how well they function. We select designs on how well they will solve adaptive problems. Natural selections then follows intelligent design . . . Absolute universal formulas are at play. Changes then come about when responses follow a pre-set formula for change. We are a bundle of intricate systems of neurons that formulate functional needs as genetic, biochemical and physiological and balance them off with evolutionary or instinctual adaptations. If we select the correct adaptation we grow and contribute to our species survival and to future discoveries made possible by new adaptive neurons not previously available.

It seems to the writer that the molecular nature of the universe sets the rules for what can or cannot be done according to pre-set formula by the creator. However, the esoteric nature of man is his spiritual nature. It seems to me that this is unique to every human being. It follows a different set of rules. Different religions express the spirit or soul in their own way.

We all make bad choices which some religions see as sins. Sin is a word that has been bantered about to the point it has different meanings. The Greek word for sin is Hamartia a word purported to be used in archery meaning to miss the point. It is also is interesting to note that the word repentance in Greek means to change perspective. Is this not then the process of seeing the point or waking up to realize have missed the point in a choice? By recognizing you have missed the point you [repent] which means you change your perspective thereby eliminating the sin of incorrect choice in future situations.

In Islam the word "Tawbah" [or Repentance] means "to return." Basically the act of leaving God and returning to what He has commanded. In other words making a wrong choice and correcting it.

According to the Gospel of Thomas, Jesus was asked by his disciples, "When will Heaven come?" He replied, "It won't come by waiting for it, because Heaven is spread out upon earth people don't see it." Jesus also said . . ."the kingdom is within you and it is outside you."

Science then is the vehicle that takes us over new roads to discoveries in the future. The human spirit chooses the road we will follow. Hopefully, one day all Religions will awaken to the realization that all roads lead to the same destination. Let's start looking for Heaven here in the world of our reality, it is in us and all around us, we are all one.

Science complements religion.

PART II

When Does Life Start?

Pro-life vs. Pro-choice

When the sperm enters the egg and blastula, cell division is initiated; we have a new creative force in our world. Over the next approximately nine months a fetus develops into a new baby. Brain, mind, soul and Holy Spirit are in place. Molecular evolution has taken place and the newborn baby at birth begins to experience worldly environment by taking its first breath. The evolution of this fetus's uterine experience is complete and the experience of this new world begins.

The newborn reacts to his or her new environment and begins making choices. The baby learns that some choices return bad results and others good. Smiling brings favorable results, so the baby smiles. The privilege of choice will remain with the child for the rest of its life.

Let's look at the arguments of pro-life and pro-choice from this perspective.

Many pro-life advocates will take the stand that if life begins at conception; we have no right to abort a fetus at any time after conception. Life is sacred and not to be denied. If true we have no right to terminate a mother's life to save the unborn child.

If the choice is the mother dies or the fetus is terminated, who makes thatchoice? The choice in such cases should be the mothers not a judge or cleric.

If the argument is, the new child should live and be able to bring new children into the world in the future, then why not let the mother live and bring other children into the world a lot sooner than a new born could?

We must all live with the choices we make but why should we be dictated by someone else's beliefs?

This is like saying if you don't convert to Islam, by someone else's choice you must be terminated.

Society has its rules and that's what makes our civilization. However in a free society, as ours, where supposedly religion does not dictate our laws, what gives certain factions the right, through their religious ideologies, to take away the God given right of choice from woman?

The right to live is fundamental but the choice to live is individual.

Every person must live by the choices they make. Agreed, every effort should be made to bring a baby to full term with preparations for adoption when agreed to by the parents.

But the final decision should be the mothers not the father who has no life risk involved.

The unborn child is the mother's responsibility not the states or some religious dictate.

The bottom line is where do we draw the line? …Why do we think we have the right to take choice away from the mother? Is her life worth less than the unborn?

There are those who say, "Who represents the unborn child if not us?"

My answer is God, not you. Who are you to make this decision? God has given the decision of a mother's potential off-spring to the mother.

Let's say someone other than the mother should decide the child should be brought to term regardless of the mother's views or problems. What if the baby grows up to be a rapist and serial killer? Will the people who forced the mother to term be around to take responsibility for this child's actions? These sanctimonious people, who decreed no one has the right to take a life, will be long gone and the families of the victims will have no recourse based on a decision they didn't make to force the birth of a murderer. They hide under the law of unintended consequences, it is not their fault.

Every life is sacred, but the responsibility for that life should be where it belongs….with the mother.

Life is sacred, so why do we kill animals and use birth prevention techniques to prevent over population of animals? Or do we mean only life of humans is sacred?

Taking a person's will or right to choose is wrong and will only lead to more governmental or religious control. Let's not forget history and Adolph Hitler's desire for a pure Aryan race through selective breeding. Is that next?

BRAIN, MIND, SOUL AND THE SPIRIT

The author proposes that every human being regardless of his or her ethnic background is born with a different DNA and unique physical characteristics. One persons DNA may be much further refined than that of another. Each brain may have the same physical characteristics but no two are the same. It follows, to the writer, that a brain that can understand and analyze better than another is one that has more operative neurons or connections that make it possible for that brain to assimilate material that another brain cannot because it has fewer neuron connections.

DNA explains why some people are malformed while others have very few physical defects. Life begins with unequal physical and mental capacities. Why do some people with physical defects rise above those who do not? We may all be born in the legal sense as equal in opportunities but obviously not equal physically or mentally.

We are all sons and daughters of the creator. God is part of everyone and everything. Projections have been made that Venus, Mercury and other planets as Earth circling the Sun will be drawn into it in 6.5 billion years and melt into oblivion. There is only an outside chance that the Earth will escape into outer space, and if it does we are told it will be a barren desolate sphere. Obviously we should start looking for a place to live while we can. With politics and humans doing what they do we will need 6.5 billion years to work out a program If one shrugs his shoulders and says, so what, I'll be in heaven or Nirvana by then, one should ask the question, where will that be? Certainly not in the physical world as we know it. If we return to the world to increase our experiences we might be around for the final destruction of the world that we thought would remain forever. The only thing that remains forever is nothing.

Let's look at the brain, mind and soul of humanity as it relates to the Holy Spirit. The brain makes a decision to choose one thing over another. A decision is made by experience and the individual's emotional and intellectual capacity. The choice made becomes a part of that individual's soul. Good or bad is irrelevant the choice made is unchangeable.

Each person's mind is driven by his or her conscious and unconscious self. A choice is made by the mind after conscious and unconscious input of the brain and the person's soul as it has developed to that point in what we call time. A choice is made. The cause begins and the reaction mental and /or physical is recorded in the brain as memory and instantaneously in that person's Soul. The soul, being part of the Spirit also records the decision. When finally all choices are made based on Love the soul returns to the unblemished state of Grace.

The Spirit is the Creator of the unending universe and the soul's connection to the Spirit is absolute since it is part of the Creator. You cannot destroy a soul because it is part of creation and the creator.

To the author science is the proof of the Creator. Yes, I believe Intelligent Design is the creator's formula for all things and that God's Creative Design of this world will be discovered by science.

Let us look at the interconnection of:

SPIRIT, SOUL, MIND, BRAIN

SPIRIT

SOUL   MIND

BRAIN

Through our senses the brain experiences what is seen, heard or felt. Your mind dictates the choice to be made. This choice and its after actions are also recorded by the Soul and the spirit. By choices we make our soul aspires to perfection which is only in the Creator. The Spirit is that part of every life touched by the Devine. Isn't this what was said in The Gospel According to Mary Magdalene . . . Chapter 5 . . . 10) I said to him, Lord, how does he who sees the vision see it, through the soul or through the spirit? 11) The Savior answered and said, He does not see through the soul nor through the spirit, but the mind that is between the two is what sees the vision and it is [. . .]

When God gave human life to mankind he also gave him an unblemished soul. Man's soul became blemished, called sin, because by the use of his brain he made wrong choices, as in the Garden of Eden. The unblemished Soul was part of perfection; man and woman must now make the choices that will be impressed upon their soul. When perfect choices through Love are finally made, the unblemished soul will again take its place as part of the Creator. Soul will become Spirit.

On the question on where does matter go after physical death we find the answer provided by The Gospel of Mary . . . P.35 . . . Will matter then be destroyed or not?

The Savior said, "All natures, all formations, all creatures exist in and with one another and they will be resolved again into their own roots. For the nature of matter is resolved into the (roots) of its nature alone. He who has ears to hear, let him hear." Gospel of Phillip . . . P.40, 4th Para. Second column. "The Christ has everything in himself; man, angel, mystery and the father."

WHERE DO WE LOOK FOR GOD?

II: Coptic Gospel of Thomas

> 15) Jesus said, When you see one who was not born of woman, prostrate yourselves on your faces and worship him. That one is your Father.

That statement covers everyone born in this world. Has the reader ever heard of any man or woman that wasn't born of woman?

If one does not follow the religious dogma of one's religion he or she becomes an outcast.

This action implies there is only one way to believe in and understand God, my way or no way.

It seems to me that most religions get so caught up in their dogma and traditional ceremonies that they have lost sight of why they were conceived in the first place. I do not believe that God is found by following one religious order. Religious orders are man's earthly conceptions.

I believe that the Creator is a part of everything. Each person has the freedom to reach for that part in him or her that is divine. God is waiting for discovery by every human being.

> Gospel of Mary . . . Page 36 . . . Lo here Lo there. For the son of man is within you. Do not lay down rules . . .

God is not found in a religion or in procedures unless something in those areas help the person to discover The Creator in him or herself.

Let us start with the physical body, which is different in every individual, move on internally to the brain, which is different in every individual, the mind operating through the brain is different in each individual, the Soul which helps direct the mind and records all the actions of the individual, which is different in each individual, and finally the Creator or Spirit which is the same in every individual.

The only thing that is the same in all of us and unchangeable is God the Creator.

One of our problems as humans is to constantly look for our connection with God down the easiest possible path. We turn to religion for the answer, to cults or any other instant answer for our lives and our actions.

If we humans could agree that the only perfection in us is that part which is the Creator, we could all strive to find God in ourselves and see him in others. This would be common ground for civilization to try to be tolerant and work with others regardless of their religious beliefs, and ethnical differences.

One may not believe the scriptures quoted above but that does not diminish the truth in the message.

THERE IS NOTHING NEW

If you believe in cause and effect that every action produces a reaction, then our words and actions create all situations in life as we know it. Many times it is difficult even impossible to understand why things occur as they do. Fair, as we understand it, does not occur in nature. The law of eat or be eaten, kill or be killed, is seen from sea life to all creatures on earth. Sympathy, empathy and time are human conceptions which hopefully are part of our human evolution in a cycle of transition from non-matter to matter to non-matter.

Science says matter can neither be made nor destroyed. We perceive each other in human form, in reality we are looking at billions of atoms lined up in a formation that distinguishes each of us as individuals, no two of us the same. But all of us composed of the same atomic material. Our molecular structure changes from conception to death and even after death.

I believe there is an unseen in all of us that is indestructible. That element is creation. We are all part of God the Creator. There is no one religion that has an inside track to God. Jews, Christians, Muslims, Buddhists, Hindus, Taoist, are all roads that lead to the same Creator. My life is what I made it given the gift of free will. My future, as yours, is based on the choices we make today.

Why do we believe we are so different? Jews, Christians and Muslims believe in one God (even though they dispute who that God is). Hindus believe there are many Gods, but of the three there is Brahma, the creator. Buddhists believe in no God but prayer through self enlightenment, New Age believe each individual is God, Sikhs (disciples) propose that God's name is "True name" who pre-destined all creatures, a Muslim teaching, this religion merged Hindu and Muslim beliefs. All theses religions lay down principles to live by which apparently work in their domain. Our problem has always been one religion trying to impose itself on others. Is it any wonder we are always having wars?

My brother, Harry C. Bay, published a book entitled, "The Key to the Universe," which delves into the unified field theory of the universe. His theory is based on findings that gravity is the binding universal force in the universe. The changing of non-mass to mass has been explored in the forms of neutrinos, a mass—less form of pure energy which can create new mass. These experiments have already taken place in England. The significance of these experiments boggles the mind.

As this theory proves out that man can transform pure energy into mass, we are only discovering what has always been . . . we are not creating something new. These experiments merely point to the unimaginable magnitude of the Creators works.

Why not have a World-wide union, Intelligent Design in Science, Religion and You.

IT'S TIME TO UNITE RELIGIONS IN A DEMOCRATIC ASSEMBLY.

Have the representatives of the world's religions meet at the United Nations Building in New York. The purpose of the meeting would be to establish a democracy of all participating religions. All religious groups attending to acknowledge the right of the other to practice their beliefs without conflict. In the United States everyone has the right to believe in whatever religion they desire without interference from others. All religions should work together to condemn far right terrorists actions.

Perhaps one day all religions will agree there is only one God and they are all praying to the same entity. In the meantime, they agree to live and let live and to pray to their own God or Allah in peace.

HERE'S A HYPOTHETICAL

What if your Soul and Spirit are on a journey?

FIVE "WHAT IFS."

In this world all animals, minerals and vegetables are made of the atoms already in this world. Someone born in this world is composed of the molecules provided him or her by the mother and father from molecules provided from the mothers egg and fathers sperm. The baby's growth at first comes from the mother's milk or some substitute. When the child begins to eat on his own he is growing by ingesting the molecules that make up his food. The child continues his or her molecular absorption until physical death. At this time the atoms and molecules return to the earth and do not travel with the soul and spirit to another place.

What if the spirit takes the soul to its next journey where if it requires materialization it draws atoms and molecules already there and is reborn and made up of molecules of that world or planet or place?

What if the purpose of this evolution is to allow every soul to grow towards perfection until it becomes one with the spirit? The molecular structure of the universe stays intact.

What if we set the premise that every soul is at a different stage of development and must experience all aspects of creation before returning to the original cause? No one knows if this is true and no one knows that it s false. In this world humans are born with a brain carrying out functions for the mind, and the mind relaying experiences to the soul.

What if the spirit permeates the brain, mind and soul and records all things?

After physical death, as we know it, our molecules return to the earth and become part of the never ending cycle of life.

What if our soul and spirit continues the journey to only where or what is known by God. If this were true would you approach life differently and respect others for their beliefs even though they are not yours? Hindu or Buddhists would all live in harmony. If all people on earth followed the same religion would wars stop? This is like saying by changing your religion you change human nature. Doesn't it make more sense to let people choose whatever religion they feel comfortable with and you do the same and live in peace? Albert Camus a French philosopher [1930-1960] said it well:

"Don't walk behind me, I may not lead. Don't walk in front of me, I may not follow. Just walk beside me and be my friend."

"To those who say it can't be done, I refer you to an old Chinese proverb."

"Those who say it cannot be done should not interrupt those who are doing it."

WE ARE ALL DESCENDANTS OF ONE GOD

We are all descendants of God the Creator. This is stated in clear terms, see Mathew 6:9. After this manner therefore pray ye: Our Father which art in heaven Hallowed be thy name. This of course is the beginning of the "Lord's Prayer" recited by Jesus himself. In Latin our father is "Pater Noster" so this prayer is sometimes called "the Paternoster."

The "Lord's Prayer does not say "My Father," or "Your Father," or the Christian, Jew or Islamic Father; it says the all inclusive "Our Father." What could be clearer?

FOR A QUICK REFERENCE TO RELIGIONS

IN THIS TEXT PLEASE REVIEW:

Religions agree with Intelligent Design.

The oneness of the universe is pointed out in many of the religions listed below. The molecular concept of science does not contradict this belief it confirms it.

Primitive People God is the ultimate law giver and overseer. He is beyond prayer and magic. Nana is an indwelling of power that can cause extraordinary actions.

Early Jewish Religion.

Moses initiated seventy elders in the secret doctrine and they transmitted it then from hand to hand. It is said that Moses de Leon compiled the Zohar [a book on cabalistic commentaries on scripture] around AD 1305.

The Quabbala . . . Is the secret hidden tradition of the unwritten law . . . delivered to man to understand the mystery of the universe about him and within him.

Hinduism [India] 800 BC

The way of knowledge . . . Jnana Marge . . . All things men, animals, plants come from one thing or being to which they return.

Taoism [China] 604-531 BCE

Tao-Te-Ching wrote . . . Treaty on the Tao and its power . . . All things come from non-being and return to non-being.

Sages know, it continues, all things come from and blend into one and that they are themselves are one with all things in the one.

All things and all natural processes are interaction between the Yang [positive], and the Yen [feminine] the passive mood. Yin is at rest

Confucius 531 BC [China] Born Confucius Kung fu-Tzu.

He taught Shu . . . do as one would be done by. He taught the doctrine of mutualality. Found in the Christians golden rule . . . Do unto others as you would have others do unto you.

Christianity 4 or 6 BC

Note: Genesis 2:7 And the Lord God formed man of the dust of the ground, and breathed into his nostrils the breath of life; and man became a living soul.

According to the Gospel of Thomas, Jesus was asked by a disciple, "When will Heaven come?" He replied, "It won't come by waiting for it, because Heaven is spread out upon earth people don't see it." Jesus also said . . ."the kingdom is within you and it is outside you."

In the Gospel of Mary Magdalene Jesus is quoted as saying, "All natures, all formed things, all creatures exist in and with one another and will again be resolved into their own roots, because the nature of matter is dissolved into the roots of its nature alone."

Doesn't it follow that Jesus was born of and through Mary of this earth, all of molecular structure. Therefore, Jesus walked this earth according to God's formulas of molecular structures.

Mohammad AD 570

The prophet was born of woman of this earth and lived in its molecular structure.

Bahai's Faith [writings of Bahaullah . . . 1817-1892]

They believe in the harmony of science and religion.

Buddhism [560 BC] India

Buddha, born of human parents, believed persons and the world is in a constant state of flux. Nothing remains immune to change but Nirvana. This world is an illusion there is no permanence.

Zen . . . Mahayana Buddhism [means great] in Japan, It is also known as Ch'an in China. 5th-6th Cent.

It presents logical paradoxes [Koans] that will cause one to give up logical explanations. One is to wait for intuition of his own Buddha's essence.

Satori . . . A key concept to Zen Buddhism

Oneness of the universal self is pre-supposed. All phenomena are alike in their Buddha essence.

Jainism . . . India . . . 6th. Century

Founder, Mahavira rejected the caste system and the practice by priests of the sacrifices of animals. He said . . . "Man, you are your own friend, why do you wish for a friend beyond yourself?" He never killed any living being. He is purported to have said, "a Man is not saved by God or a priest but by his own efforts.